The

GW01003284

Progress Along the Way:
Life, Service and Realization

SEVEN STAR
COMMUNICATIONS
Santa Monica, CA

SevenStar Communications Group, Inc.
1314 Second Street
Santa Monica, California 90401

Copyright 1994 by Hua-Ching Ni.

First Printing August 1994

Acknowledgments: Thanks and appreciation to Suta Cahill, Janet DeCourtney and Tiane Sommer for assistance in organizing, editing and producing this booklet.

It is recommended that you study Hua-Ching Ni's other books and materials for further knowledge about a healthy lifestyle and to learn other practices. There are no claims for absolute effectiveness of the material in this booklet, which is to be used at your own discretion.

Contents

Foreword

This booklet is for all who wish to work together to improve themselves as part of the one great life of the world. Here is succinct guidance for your progress in daily life, service to others, and realization of the Integral Way in your life and service.

For those who have been using my books for many years, these concise outlines are sufficient because your understanding has broadened and deepened. No plant can grow on distilled water alone, however, and especially if you are a new reader you might need to read my other books to fully understand this material.

This material was delivered at the Gateless Gate Retreat in San Destin, Florida in spring, 1994 as the foundation for Mentors working together as a team. The participants, Mentors of the Integral Way, use the teachings of the Integral Way as a model for their own lives and volunteer to help promote the Universal Integral Way. All of them have my deep appreciation. Some participants suggested that Sage Yellow Stone's precious instruction should be the constitution of the Universal Society of the Integral Way. This suggestion was warmly received.

Your sincerity has earned my lifelong dedication, and your dedication will nourish your growing ability to help yourself and help the world.

Hua-Ching Ni

Part One

I
The Universal Awareness of All People

All spiritual individuals should recognize their social responsibility to give spiritual help. Social and cultural trends in the modern world are confused and negative. Most people are confused about the value of life. Their good judgment has been usurped by emotional indulgence, a misleading commercial culture, and the narrow prejudice of religions that offer no real spiritual development.

Working correctly in the mainstream of life is an important spiritual service. The guiding power of such service should be the association between the developed mind and the achieved soul of all people which contains love, rationality, conscience and everlasting values.

In practical terms, the principle behind social-spiritual service of the Integral Way is to pay attention to attain our own spiritual well-being and extend that well-being to help other people. Pay attention to the quality of your service. Allow your social development to rely on the principle of naturalness.

When you work in a group you can have ideas and make suggestions, but do not be opinionated. Most people are not selfish, but they are opinionated at times. One should be aware of this and correct oneself. Being opinionated is a problem of thinking too highly of oneself and too little of others. To a spiritual individual, to stubbornly hold onto an opinion is a mark of spiritual undevelopment and creates disharmony.

In group leadership, being reasonable is in the broad interests of the majority. The purpose of a group effort is to benefit all people, the majority and the minority alike. The well-being of society as a whole is the ultimate goal. No benefit should be limited to either the majority or minority of any group of people. It is unrighteous to impose the democratic vote of an inconsiderate or short-sighted majority on everyone. It is spiritually correct to recognize that one clear-minded individual is worth thousands of people who are self-interested and short-sighted.

When you do something that is visibly good, pay attention to the invisible atmosphere, particularly in a society. Each person learns at least one art and one skill and becomes good at them. You build your conscience in this way rather than depending on something or someone else to tell you what to do and how to do it. As a spiritual individual, you clearly know that some old customs need to be corrected or perhaps totally altered.

A. There should be a worldwide spiritual awareness that the human population needs to move in the direction of:

1) a gentle approach to life, but with spiritual self-strengthening

2) worldwide spiritual integration

3) a healthy lifestyle

4) good customs and activities

5) wholesome rituals, civility and protective self-discipline

6) broad spiritual education and service

7) mutual assistance at different levels of life

B.   A spiritual individual should help friends of good character and good capability by:

1) offering help, but not trying to control

2) never being jealous of a friend's good character or capability

3) helping friends to develop as highly or higher than oneself

4) knowing one's limitations

C.   A spiritual individual should develop the following attitudes toward teaching:

1) to serve as a spiritual assistant of society

2) to accept all friends who wish to engage in spiritual learning

3) to accept and gather all good reinterpretations of old customs and backward cultural trends

4) to work together with people of the same aspiration to restore a broad faith in the universal Divine One and in universal life

5) to filter out all cultural confusion that is unfit for natural life

6) to unite people of spiritual conscience and of universal consciousness for the promotion of a universal society

7) to move wholeheartedly in the new direction of realizing the path of universal conscience

D. An individual of universal conscience should observe the following guidelines for social behavior and activity:

1) respect your moral obligation to your parents, family and children

2) respect and recognize the convention of marriage

3) be careful in your choice of sexual partners so that you do not cause trouble for yourself or the other person

4) keep your sexual activity private; do not attempt to influence public opinion with your views on sexual matters

5) respect your sexual partner by simplifying your sexual relationship and reward him or her with material support in order to avoid sexual abuse

6) communicate responsibly with your partner; do not harass him or her

7) do not become a sexual partner with anyone who is directly involved with your work

8) learn and practice gentle martial arts in place of the fighting impulse

9) take only what is fair from people

10) make money honestly in an ethical way, spend money wisely, and manage your money with virtue

11) conduct a Sunday service for no charge

12) offer classes for a fair charge or no charge; a teacher should be a person of fairness

13) do not develop any teaching material that would conflict with the spirit of social dedication or the policy of fair self-support

14) do not engage in any use of drugs or alcohol

15) participate in study groups as well as individual self-study, for both support individual spiritual development and the spiritual welfare of the world

A spiritual connection with divine energy is established when you are motivated to learn the truth and straighten yourself out. You should not engage in fanatic faith or worship, secret initiation, or secret obligations to a group or teacher, but instead work on your own spiritual well-being in everyday life.

Spiritual salvation is a privilege earned by your own effort to learn the Integral Way and live up to it. It is true that all people's spiritual nature is sufficient and that any darkness should be removed by your own effort.

- No one should think that their life can be a flowering plant in a glass house.
- At the same time you are living in the world, you should be reflecting on the subtle reality of your life and studying the Integral Way.
- You realize life in each moment that you discover the Universal Divine One within you; otherwise, you lose it.

The Universal Divinity is what you have gone through, the spiritual awareness you have attained, and how you continue your spiritual accomplishment to join with all spiritually developed ones of the past, present and future.

II
The Call of Universal Conscience

1

Each individual was born with their own perfection.
In the architecture of human society,
_   each person has a good use._
The long is what mends the short.
The short is what mends the long.
The perfection of the entire building
_   is the health and wealth of society._

2

That is to say:
Nature gives birth to people
_   whose natures are perfect in different ways._

It is important to know that
   all people have something that is long
   and also something that is short.
You need to develop self-observation
   in order to attain accurate self-knowledge.
Then you will know what is long and short
   in yourself.
You will also know that you need help
   from other people
   and you need to help other people.
Both require a cooperative attitude or personality.

You need to apply what is long in yourself
   to assist what is short in others,
   appreciate what is long in others,
   and mend what is short yourself.
As each learns to accept the other,
   a good life is attained for all,
   and a healthy and prosperous society is born.

3

There is no need to fight among yourselves.
There is no need to compete against one another
   for selfish motives.

Each individual should develop oneself.
Each individual should offer the best use of oneself
in a conjoint effort and constructive direction.
A natural life means to accomplish oneself.
A social life means to accomplish a common goal
through perfect cooperation.

4

Since hardly anyone is perfect,
let all people learn together
and assist one another to live a better life
and have a better world.
Do not forget:
each person's spiritual development
is the key to real progress
in oneself and in the world.

5

Do you know the story of two people,
one of whom is weak-sighted
and the other who has difficulty walking?
They helped each other through life.
Once there was a fire in their neighborhood,
and their dwelling started to burn.

The way out of the building was difficult.
After conferring quickly,
  the one who was poor at walking
  climbed on the back of the weak-sighted one.
Through cooperation, they safely escaped.
This story illustrates the one reality of life.
Self-reliance is the practice of personal life,
  but interdependence is required
  to attain a common goal.

6

Do you know the story of an old man
  who had many sons and daughters?
They argued with one another constantly.
The family did not improve a bit,
  year after year.
One day, the old man summoned each child to him.
He gave each one an arrow
  and asked them to break it.
Each one did it easily.
Then the old man took an entire handful of arrows
  and asked each one to break the bunch.
But none was able to do so.

I ask you, children of nature,
*   would you like to be single and broken*
*   by the dangerous trends of the world?*
Or would you prefer to unite on the uncharted voyage
*   to guard yourselves and others*
*   from the vicious wind and waves?*

7

My interest is not to take anything from the world.
My interest is to give what is needed.
I encourage you to move in a direction
*   where there is work and enjoyment.*
The map I draw for you
*   is of the uncharted voyage of the human race.*
It shows the way out of the mist.

I ask you
*   to break through the separation of all religions*
*   and find the spiritual origin.*

I ask you
*   to remove the hostility between all races*
*   and reunite all people as one family.*

I ask you
    to cleanse degenerate social customs and practices
    and restore the natural spiritual purity life.

I ask you
    to promote universal spiritual unity
    and correct all spiritual divergence.

I ask you
    to straighten crooked cultures
    and attain healthy lives.

I ask you
    to move toward universal friendship
    and cooperation
    and dissolve all wars and aggression.

I ask you
    to build a harmonious universal society
    and restore natural happiness.

I ask you
    to bring Heaven to Earth
    by correcting all religious fantasies.

I request you
   to enliven the spirits within you
   and invigorate
   the natural foundation of your lives.

I request you
   to realize internal and external spiritual integration
   and achieve health and longevity.

I request you
   to continue the life of universal life.

I request you
   to take nutrition from high wisdom.

I request you
   to apply reason
   in selecting your lifestyle.

I request you
   to consult the universal conscience within you
   and respond to the mission I give to you,
   which is to build
   the Universal Society of the Integral Way.

When this reality is reached
   the name should be discarded.

To be forever with the Way
   is to take nothing from the world,
   but to give back what the world should have,
   which has either been stolen from people
   or lost by people themselves.

III
Basic Spiritual Guidance and Practice
of the Universal Integral Way

1. Value an undisturbed mind at all times.
   • See *The Complete Works of Lao Tzu* and *Attaining Unlimited Life*

2. Appreciate and repay favors.
   • See *The Key to Good Fortune*

3. Depart from perplexity; work to achieve clarity.
   •See *Tao: The Subtle Universal Law, Guide t Inner Light*, and *Moonlight in the Dark Night*

4. Accept the changes of the external world. Maintain peacefulness within yourself.
> • See *The Book of Changes and the Unchanging Truth*

5. Do not take trouble personally if the trouble is not created by you or cannot be avoided.
> • See *The Key to Good Fortune*

6. Pay attention to the conditions of life and the things that are related to you. Try to reform the conditions in order to obtain good results.
> • See *The Key to Good Fortune*

7. Form no conceptual justification for your emotions.
> • See the *Hua Hu Ching* (in *The Complete Works of Lao Tzu*) and *Moonlight in the Dark Night*

8. Take on no burdens. Avoid doing anything wrong.
> • See *The Key to Good Fortune* and *Tao: The Subtle Universal Law*

9. Stay calm and self-composed at all times.
> • See *The Complete Works of Lao Tzu* and *Attaining Unlimited Life*

10. Rarefy your extra desires.
> • See *The Complete Works of Lao Tzu*

11. Remain simple.
> • See *The Complete Works of Lao Tzu*

12.   Protect your spiritual unity and nourish your vital energy.
> • See *Workbook for Spiritual Development of All People* and *Strength from Movement: Mastering Chi.*

13.   Unite with the health of nature.
> • See *The Complete Works of Lao Tzu* and *Attaining Unlimited Life*

14.   Practice Dao-In and strengthen your vitality.
> • See *Attune Your Body with Dao-In* and all other movement books and videos.

15.   Gather good energy. Choose if possible to live in a good, natural environment; visit places that have good energy; learn the breathing system from the booklets "Guide to Your Total Well-Being" and "The Light of All Stars Illuminates the Way"; and learn a form of gentle exercise. When you do anything in a good environment, it is also a way to take in good energy. All of these will support your physical health and spiritual growth. If you read my books, you will also receive good energy from them. In general, you should learn to guard your energy, not contaminate it by destructive thoughts or images.
> • See *Strength from Movement: Mastering Chi*, *Workbook for Spiritual Development* and the *Heavenly Way* booklet

6. Control your eating and drinking.
   - See *The Tao of Nutrition*

7. Be centered and balanced in all matters.
   - See *The Book of Changes and Unchanging Truth*

8. Be kind, appropriate, civil; trustworthy and wise.
   - See *The Key to Good Fortune* and *Stepping Stones for Spiritual Success*

19. Dissolve your own hypocrisy.
   - See *The Complete Works of Lao Tzu*

20. Learn to recognize the subtle natural response.
   - See *Tao: The Subtle Universal Law*

21. Observe the subtle law.
   - See *The Key to Good Fortune*

22. Respect the Way and fulfill the nature of life.
   - See *The Complete Works of Lao Tzu and Attaining Unlimited Life*

23. Create no problems.
   - See *The Complete Works of Lao Tzu, Attaining Unlimited Life, The Story of Two Kingdoms* and the *Heavenly Way* booklet

24. Do do not harm yourself spiritually. Promote the spiritual benefit of all.
   - See *The Key to Good Fortune*

25. Respect virtuous people.
    • See *The Key to Good Fortune*

26. Respect spiritual harmony.
    • See *The Key to Good Fortune*

27. Unite virtue with good laws to guide yourself and your subordinates.
    • See *The Key to Good Fortune* and *Stepping Stones for Spiritual Success*

28. Unite righteousness with profit making.
    • See *The Key to Good Fortune*

29. Accept the universe as your own being.
    • See *Majestic Domain of Universal Heart*

30. Do not be extreme in anything.
    • See *The Book of Changes and the Unchanging Truth*

31. Know the cycle of history.
    • See *The Book of Changes and the Unchanging Truth*

32. Use gentle words, gentle means, gentle thought and gentle behavior.
    • See *The Complete Works of Lao Tzu*

33. Live in harmony with the natural world.
    • See *Attaining Unlimited Life*

34. Be open to learning what is good, and refuse bad influence from any aspect of society.
   • See _The Integral Way of Life_

35. Practice self-control.
   a) Align the mind, body and soul through a light diet. - _Su Chai_
   b) Align the mind, body and soul through eating less. - _Chieh Shih Chai_
   c) Align the mind, body and soul through methodic fasting. - _Tien Shih Chai_
   d) Align the mind, body and soul through mental purification. - _Shing Chai_

During the summer, physical cleansing may be done by a fruit or vegetable fast, beginning around the time of the Summer Solstice (June 21/22 in the Northern Hemisphere or December 21/22 in the Southern Hemisphere). A fast can be suitable if it feels right for your body or you consult your physician.

During the hot days of the summer, it is best to stop eating beef or lamb and increase your consumption of fruits and vegetables. You can eat more beef and lamb in the winter, and you can also increase your use of onions, garlic, ginger, leeks and other warming foods at that time.

36. In the hot seasons, be temperate in food and alcohol. In the cold seasons, be temperate in sex. Sexual activity is suitable in hot weather. Alcohol is suitable in cold weather.

Note: The above references to see specific books are only suggested reading. Each of Hua-Ching Ni's books presents the Integral Way.

IV
Universal Authentic Persons:
The Essential Example of the
Ancient Wise Ones

The ancient wise one retreats from
glamour and excitement.

The ancient wise one retreats from
competition for immediate benefit.

The ancient wise one retreats from
contention and dispute.

The ancient wise one retreats from
involvement in possibly controversial matters.

The ancient wise one retreats from
negative arguments or fights.

The ancient wise one retreats from
any opportunity for selfish gain.
He or she goes where
there is opportunity to help others.

The ancient wise one has no interest in
social struggles of unclear intention.

The ancient wise one respects
a life of peace and serenity above all else.
He or she moves quietly
toward the positive aspects of life.

The ancient wise one chooses great tasks
that other people would forsake.
He or she accepts pressure
in order to restore the health of the world.

The ancient wise ones were free when
they entered life and they are free to choose to go.
They know to effectively accomplish their tasks.

The ancient wise one lives selflessly
in order to accept and unite with the universal spirit.

The ancient wise one advocates a lifestyle
that stands on the shore of human society
without swimming in the whirlpool of human history.

Only people on the shore are able to see
and shout to those who are struggling
and have lost all other choice but drowning.
An authentic person is the lifeline
for someone caught in the whirlpool of worldly life.
Oh swimmer, hold up your hand!

V
The Model of Universal Great Life

1. *It is of great spiritual benefit
   to keep a low profile in life.*

2. *It is a great spiritual fulfillment to take no credit
   for the meaningful task you are doing.*

3. *It is of great spiritual benefit,
   if you are successful in your life or work
   and you make no noise about it.*

4. *It is of great spiritual benefit,
   if you have failed to achieve a better life or work,
   to accept it as your learning process.*

5. *It is of great spiritual benefit,*
    when you pursue success in life,
    not to play tricks.

6. *It is a great spiritual advance,*
    when you pursue spiritual achievement,
    to make no negative sacrifice
    of the duties of normal life.

7. *It is a great spiritual power*
    to calmly accept the pressures
    of well-purposed work and a moral life.

8. *It is wise to react*
    to the challenges of society and of work
    by responding only to what is meaningful.

9. *It is wisdom that enables you to respond*
    to hostile people without confrontation.

10. *It is spiritual growth that allows you*
    to not complain about the uncontrollable past
    as "karma," but to consider
    the natural or rational social causes.

11. *It is of spiritual benefit, whenever*
    your mind is disturbed by emotional matters,

to accept them as a test
and maintain a poised mind and self-possession.

12. _It is a sign of spiritual maturity that you
may be able to become suddenly rich or famous,
or may have a sudden romantic attraction,
without losing your center.
If you think your success is due to good karma,
however, you will only lose it faster._

13. _It is wisdom always to keep in mind
what Lao Tzu said:
When you do more for people, you find in the end
you have done much more for yourself.
When you do not participate in the race
for success, you outrun all your competitors._

14. _It is a spiritual achievement to realize
a big ego is a sign of immaturity
that causes difficulty in work
and in other useful forms of cooperation.
Only when the ego dies does the true God emerge
from the furry hide of the beast._

15. _It is a sign of spiritual growth
to remember what Lao Tzu said:
If false sages do not cease to appear,_

*evil leaders will continue to come forth
to rob and persecute people,
because false teachings create
the theoretical foundation for evil to thrive.*

16. *It is a truthful spiritual fulfillment
that if you are doing the work of a messiah,
you accomplish it without proclaiming it.
If you are doing the work of a savior,
you do it without claiming it as your own.
If you are doing the work of the messenger,
you announce the unadorned truth
without announcing yourself.
You let all immature games of society pass you by.
You let only good spiritual work come from you.*

VI
A Universal Individual Should
Avoid Making the Following Mistakes

1. Thinking of yourself too much, and too little
   about the people who are related to you.

2. Being overly self-confident.

3. Being proud, arrogant and self-aggrandizing.

4. Being greedy for high position and reward.

5. Being greedy for money and extra possessions.

6. Lacking precision and good timing in response to situations.

7. Lacking the courage to make a move for moral reasons.

8. Not keeping your word.

9. Lacking prudence in your actions.

10. Responding too slowly.

11. Being brave but having no real strength.

12. Being indecisive by nature.

13. Having no self-discipline or ability to discipline others.

14. Neglecting your duty.

15. Being cruel to subordinates.

16. Abusing power.

17. Being selfish and self-serving in a common effort.

18. Creating confusion by changing your mind too often and too much.

19. Being overly concerned with control and having no trust in subordinates.

20. Not knowing how to make full use of other people's cooperation.

21. Lacking an accurate understanding of obstacles.

22. Having no base of support.

23. Having self-pity.

24. Showing too many shortcomings.

25. Not knowing the Way, which is love for people and the righteousness of life.

VII
What a Leader Should Not Do

The word "leader" is general. Everyone leads their own life, and is called upon to exercise leadership in various ways in family life, social life, managing money, work, and making decisions for yourself in aspects of individual life. Leadership does not necessarily carry a title; people often develop and exercise leadership ability before being asked to fill a position. Also, if you find yourself under a leader who has difficulties, instead of giving up you can exercise leadership capability in a supportive way.

The following principles are basic to achieving success in family, finance, and leadership at any level. They are all practical suggestions that you might find useful in your life.

1. Make a wrong move. *When you should move forward, you move backward. When you should move backward, you move forward.*

2. Use the wrong people or wrong material and trust them as the supportive power. *People who are confused; seeking escape; self-defeating; or, improper material; improper use of the right material.*

3. Allow unceasing disputes in yourself
   or among your people.

4. Take no decisive direction.

5. Not carry through on a decision. *No unified action.*

6. Permit people's lack of obedience and faithfulness.

7. Lose the support of the broader base.

8. Take too long to bolster morale.

9. Become too thoughtful of things and people.
   Create an emotional drawback.

10. Incur too much loss and unsupported elements.

11. Have no clear goal, or a goal that is indirect.
    Causes self-weakening.

12. Suffer an emotional shock caused by life
    or by self-disturbance.

13. Create difficulties in making a useful maneuver.

14. Have no well-organized force to support
    the widely benefitting plan.

15. Lack unification among different forces.

16. Become exhausted from overwork.
    Fail to renew necessary resources.

17. Pay too much attention to defensive aspects so
    the power to carry out the project is weakened.

18. Set no security measures.

19. Change a decision repeatedly.

20. Allow the mind to dissipate,
    so that the inner leadership is not respected.

21. Allow inner leadership to be partial to something.
    Cause emotional unacceptance of the whole being.

22. Hesitate so followers do not know what to follow.

23. Be unwilling to listen to criticism or comment.

24. Make use of incapable people
    just because of a close personal relationship.

25. Give away information that should not
    be given away. *Cause morale to fall.*

26. Make no clear decision
    when the occasion requires it.

27. Expect the fall of others, or hope to succeed
    by being lucky.

28. Depend on a scheme to command forces
    which have no trust in the action.

29. Have no preventive measure
    as part of the plan of action.

30. Have a fear of action itself.

31. Stay too long in a hostile region.

32. Allow the abuse of authority
    in disrespectful subordinates who would
    administer unfair punishment to others.

33. Apply a regular approach to an irregular situation.

34. Coordinate people, tools
    and other conditions poorly.

35. Apply too much self-restraint in using power.

36. Fear some aspect of your duty as leader,
    and thereby create a vacancy or blind spot
    of inattention.

Part Two

The following work is from Sage Yellow Stone's precious instruction. Sage Yellow Stone was the reclusive teacher of Chahng Liang, who opposed the violent reign of the first Emperor of Chin (248-246 B.C.) and helped establish the Han Dynasty (206 B.C.-219 A.D.). The great recluse gave this treatise to Chahng Liang.

I
The Main Direction

1. *The Way is universal truth. Realizing self-development through being virtuous and kind, proper and civil assists you in achieving a great life. All five of these are needed to fulfill a complete life:*

   > *The Way*
   > *Virtue*
   > *Kindness*
   > *Propriety*
   > *Civility*

2. *The Way is what the wise one follows.*
   The Way allows all things to be as they are and fulfill their natures.

3. *Virtue enables you to prosper*
   and allows all people to fulfill their desires
   without harming one another.

4. *Kindness earns the trust and friendliness*
   of others.
   It enables all people to grow together.

5. *Propriety guides one's conduct*
   according to what is right.
   It leads one to withdraw from wrongdoing.
   This is how to accomplish
   a natural and healthy life.

6. *Civility enables you to live*
   with your family and society,
   where you fulfill your duty
   and learn to tolerate differences.

These are the foundation of a universally healthy personality and a life that is complete.

7. *Wise and gentle people clearly understand*
   what brings prosperity, what causes decline,
   what enables success,
   and what results in failure.

8. *They clearly understand the trends of society*
    which lead to order or disarray.
  With deep perception, they know
    where and how to offer themselves,
    and where and what to withdraw.

9. *One who knows*
    when it is not the right time or purpose
    to apply one's talent and capability
    is able to live quietly
    and embrace the universal life within.

10. *When it is the right time and right purpose,*
    one's capability and talent
    are fully dedicated to accomplishing
    the great task of spiritual development
    of all people.

11. *When the time is wrong,*
    and the goal is confused,
    one enjoys one's own nature
    and keeps to oneself.

12. *Wise and gentle people have characters*
    that are high and firm.
    Their lives are models for generations to come.

II
Self-Measurement

13. *Heaven endows you with an enduring soul.*
    The stars endow you with a brilliant mind.
    The earth endows you with a good body.
    You were raised by your parents
    *   or people functioning as parents.*
    Your life is indebted to nature.
    It is your natural obligation to help the world,
    *   especially at a time*
    *   when people are confused*
    *   and have lost their direction in life.*

14. *Few people are born wise.*
    Most people must learn to be wise.
    Are you willing to develop yourself?

15. *To achieve yourself as a model of nature:*
    *   neglect no duty of your life,*
    *   make no excuses, do only what is right,*
    *   do not rush to reap gain when it is not right,*
    *   and do not try to escape trouble*
    *   when it is right to face it.*
    If you do all of these, you will be
    *   a model of healthy, natural life.*

16. *As a model of healthy, natural life,*
    continue to develop yourself.
    Make your behavior
    a good example to others.
    Use your wisdom to avoid contact
    with the confused trends of society.
    Use your faithfulness to follow good rules.
    Be trustworthy with public duty
    or other people's money.
    If you do all of these,
    you will be a model for all people.
    Even so, you can develop yourself
    still further.

17. *In achieving mastery of life,*
    if your virtue is accepted
    even by those who are far away,
    if your competence is recognized by many,
    if your perception reflects
    all the past experience of the world,
    if your clarity can guide people
    out of confusion,
    you have achieved mastery
    of your spiritual capability.

III
Self-Preparation

18. *Restrain special interest*
    and rarefy your desire
    in order to reduce personal burden.

19. *Suppress improper impulses*
    and correct your mistakes
    in order to prevent trouble.

20. *Not drinking for fun*
    and not indulging in sex
    will preserve your health.

21. *Avoid doing what would cause suspicion*
    and keep away from what is suspect
    in order to avoid
    foolish and needless involvement.

22. *Good behavior and helpful words*
    are the way to cultivate yourself.

23. *Broad learning and deep research*
    are the way to expand your wisdom.

24. *Respecting others and moderating yourself*
    are the way to make your life secure.

25. *Deep thinking and foresight*
    make you inexhaustible.

26. *Befriending the kind and straightforward*
    keeps you from falling.

27. *Forgive the shortcomings of others,*
    correct your own shortcomings,
    be earnest in your own behavior,
    and you will be at peace with all people.

28. *Assign the capable and employ the talented*
    in order to achieve a goal.

29. *Listen to no evil talk and reject calumny*
    to put an end to confusion.

30. *Credit the source, and commemorate teachers,*
    in order not to be perplexed.

31. *Assess a matter in the beginning.*
    Then re-evaluate the whole thing.
    This will handle any emergency.

32. *Find the way to change
    and adopt what is applicable
    in order to untie knots of trouble.*

33. *Give back to people
    what they themselves produce
    in order to do no wrong.*

34. *Be firm and at the same time flexible, as
    appropriate, in order to make a real contribution.*

35. *Be cautious and careful
    in order to protect yourself.*

IV
Self-Fulfillment

36. *There is no advantage more advantageous
    than good planning.*

37. *There is no peace more peaceful
    than restraining one's impulses.*

38. *There is no urgency more urgent
    than attaining one's virtue.*

39. *There is no happiness happier
than doing good.*

40. *There is no power more powerful
than sincerity.*

41. *There is no clearness clearer
than refusing to be involved
in anything contaminated.*

42. *There is no blessing more blessed
than self-contentment.*

43. *There is no confusion more confused
than having too many interests.*

44. *There is no sadness more saddening
than the scatteredness
of one's life essence.*

45. *There is no defect more defective
than lacking constancy.*

46. *There is no deficiency more deficient
than rampant greed.*

47. *There is no darkness darker
    than unbridled ambition.*

48. *There is no isolation more isolating
    than self-righteousness.*

49. *There is no danger more dangerous than
    assigning someone you doubt to a task.*

50. *There is no failure so certain
    as someone who is selfish
    attempting to fulfill a public duty.*

V
Self-Trusteeship

Guard yourself against self-failure by knowing the following:

51. *Showing off how much you know
    reveals your shallowness.*

52. *Knowing nothing about your faults
    and shortcomings
    reveals your ignorance.*

53. *Pulling in the wrong direction*
    without making a timely correction
    reveals your bewilderment.

54. *Inviting resentment*
    by your communication
    makes trouble and enemies.

55. *Conflict between what you ask people to do*
    and your real intentions
    reveals your inefficiency.

56. *Giving an order that contradicts*
    an order you gave before
    invites argument.

57. *Expressing anger without having power*
    invites attack by others.

58. *Humiliating others in public*
    invites revenge.

59. *Giving power to those*
    who have been humiliated by you
    invites danger.

60. *Disrespecting those*
    whom you should respect
    breeds trouble.

61. *If one cooperates with people on the surface*
    but does not cooperate in fact,
    one must struggle alone in the end.

62. *Courting flatterers*
    and shunning those who are loyal
    invites self-ruin.

63. *Pursuing the attractive*
    and withdrawing from the virtuous
    is to live in the dark.

64. *Trusting only those who are close to you*
    plants no root in the public trust.

65. *Allowing a private relationship*
    to interfere in public affairs
    causes disorder.

66. *Having followers and subordinates*
    who do not work with you wholeheartedly
    will cause you to sink.

67. *For superior and subordinate to compete*
    disables their ability to function
    as a unit.

68. *For superior and subordinate*
    not to appreciate each other
    produces no achievement.

69. *For superior and subordinate*
    to be in the wrong order
    brings decline.

70. *Mistreating the weak weakens your power.*

71. *Holding a position higher than*
    one's real capability
    exhausts oneself.

72. *Having regard for your own benefit*
    while disregarding the benefit of those
    who work with you
    is self-abandon.

73. *Destroying the big merit*
    for the sake of small interest
    makes you small.

74. *To employ people but not trust them*
weakens their support.

75. *To reward the meritorious unwillingly*
disappoints people.

76. *To promise more but give less*
causes resentment.

77. *To guide people with virtue*
gathers people of similar interests.

78. *To control people*
with the threat of punishment
drives away the wise.

79. *To insist on a small complaint*
nurtures big hatred.

80. *Not appreciating small help*
obstructs big help from coming.

81. *To accept flattery*
and enjoy it like a delicious dish
but dislike admonition
will destroy you.

82. *To enjoy what one has*
    is safety.

83. *To covet other people's possessions*
    is thievery.

84. *To give a little but expect a big return*
    brings no response.

85. *To forget hard times*
    when you become well-off
    brings short joy.

86. *To remember someone's old problem*
    and neglect their new contribution
    is to clash.

87. *Making the wrong use of the right people*
    is hopeless.

88. *To force people to work for you*
    is to keep no one.

VI
Self-Security

89. *Blessings are the accumulation*
    of good spiritual qualities.

90. *Misfortune is the accumulation*
    of bad spiritual qualities.

91. *Starving is the result of disrespect*
    for hard work.

92. *Freezing is the result of prolonged idleness.*

93. *Safety is earned*
    by befriending the right people.

94. *Danger comes from losing the support*
    of good friends.

95. *Prosperity is built by constant preparation.*

96. *Poverty is created by remaining*
    behind the tide and the time.

97. *If the superior has no constant principle,*
    the subordinate is confused.

98. *Disrespecting a superior invites insecurity.*

99. *Mistrusting a subordinate blocks cooperation.*

100. *If you disrespect the people*
     who are by your side,
     those who are at a distance
     will slight you.

101. *One who has self-doubt*
     will doubt all others.
     One who has good self-confidence
     will be confident of others.

102. *Crooked people make no straight friends.*
     A crooked superior
     chooses no straight subordinates.

103. *A dangerous government*
     has no responsible ministers.
     Bad politics has no good leaders.

104. *One who loves people deeply*
     is thirsty to give help
     to well-intending people.

105. *One who is happy with a good leader*
     is willing to offer support.

106. *It is a sign of society's decline*
     when responsible people
     are not in the right positions.

107. *It is a sure sign of the fall of a society*
     when virtuous people do not stay
     and participate.

108. *Hatred remains*
     if small trouble is not forgiven.

109. *Trouble is ahead if there is no correct plan.*

110. *Where the soil is thin,*
     no big tree can grow.

111. *Where the water is shallow,*
     no big fish can live.

112. *When a tree offers no shade or thick leaves,*
big birds do not stay.

113. *Where the forest is thin,*
no big animals live.

114. *A mountain will collapse*
from its own steepness.

115. *A lake will flood*
by its own overflow.

The following advice is for building your spiritual depth and breadth.

116. *One who discards the precious stone*
has not seen it.

117. *A sheep uses the hide of a tiger*
to express the power it lacks.

118. *To pick up your jacket by the collar*
instead of the sleeve or the hem
is to know the orderly way
of doing things.

119. *To watch the ground as you walk
is to guard against stumbling
in work and in life.*

120. *When the pillars are rotten,
the house cannot stand.*

121. *When leaders are selfish
society is endangered.*

122. *When the feet are cold,
the circulation is blocked.*

123. *When people doubt the government
society is shaken.*

124. *When a mountain is going to collapse
the base is first to sink.*

125. *When leaders compete evilly
with one another,
society will decline.*

126. *When the root is withered,
the tree will dry up.*

127. *When society is sick,*
     people must suffer.

128. *To follow the vehicle in front of you*
     as it falls off the road
     is to repeat the same dangerous mistake.

129. *To support a corrupt government*
     is to be wiped out sooner.

130. *Good knowledge of past trouble*
     makes one careful of the future.
     It is wise not to repeat a mistake.

131. *One who heeds danger attains safety.*

132. *One who fears being wiped out*
     survives.

133. *Blessings come to the one who creates them.*
     It is not God's decision.
     It is the Subtle Universal Law.

134. *Trouble comes to the one who creates it.*
     It is not God's decision.
     It is the Subtle Universal Law.

135. *One who always heeds good guidance*
     does no wrong.

136. *One who can see far*
     has no immediate trouble.

137. *People's tendencies differ.*
     The brave can go forward
       but are unable to keep still.
     The conservative can hold up well
       but hesitate to go forward.
     The greedy mind can be applied
       to make progress, but cannot be made
       to share the profit with another.

138. *The incorruptible can be accountable*
     for money, but may be too inflexible
     in situations that need
     a dynamic personality.

139. *The honest can follow regular rules*
     but they may be too inflexible
     to handle an emergency.

140. *Few people are completely endowed*
with all talents.
Your own self-education
and spiritual cultivation
can mend your shortcomings.

141. *While you are liberal,*
can you also be conservative?

142. *While you are moving forward,*
can you also retreat?

143. *While you are greedy*
in making acquisitions
can you also be generous enough
to share?

144. *While you are honest in keeping rules,*
can you also be flexible
in an emergency?

145. *If you are able to be all things,*
there is sure to be success in your life
and you can offer great help to the world.

146. *May all people be equipped*
     with the good knowledge that:
     It is hard to argue with nature.
     It is a blessing to follow the Way
       of balance between self and nature.
     It is a misfortune to deviate from the Way,
       whatever you are.

The information in this booklet was written by Hua-Ching Ni based upon the teachings of the Integral Way. Some selected books by Hua-Ching Ni include:

Personal Useful and Practical Development
Power of Natural Healing
Harmony: The Art of Life
Attune Your Body with Dao-In
Strength From Movement: Mastering Chi

Fundamental Readings
Stepping Stones for Spiritual Success
The Gentle Path of Spiritual Progress
The Key to Good Fortune: Refining Your Spirit
Golden Message

Spiritual Classics
The Book of Changes and the Unchanging Truth
The Complete Works of Lao Tzu
The Esoteric Tao Teh Ching
The Taoist Inner View of the Universe
Tao: The Subtle Universal Law
The Workbook for Spiritual Development of all People

Esoteric Teachings
The Way, the Truth and the Light
Life and Teaching of Two Immortals: Master Chen Tuan
Life and Teaching of Two Immortals: Master Kou Hong
The Story of Two Kingdoms
Internal Alchemy: The Natural Way to Immortality
Mysticism: Empowering the Spirit Within

Other materials available from SevenStar Communications on natural healing arts and sciences include:

Books
The Tao of Nutrition by Dr. Maoshing Ni
Chinese Vegetarian Delights by Lily Chuang
Chinese Herbology Made Easy by Dr. Maoshing Ni
Crane Style Chi Gong by Dr. Daoshing Ni
101 Vegetarian Delights by Lily Chuang and Cathy McNease

Videotapes (VHS)
Attune Your Body with Dao-In by Hua-Ching Ni
T'ai Chi Chuan: An Appreciation by Hua-Ching Ni
Crane Style Chi Gong by Dr. Daoshing Ni
Self-Healing Chi Gong by Dr. Maoshing Ni
Eight Treasures by Dr. Maoshing Ni
T'ai Chi Chuan I & II by Dr. Maoshing Ni

Audiotapes (by Dr. Maoshing Ni)
Invocations: Health, Longevity & Healing a Broken Heart
Chi Gong for Stress Release
Chi Gong for Pain Management

For a list of other booklets or a complete catalog of books, videos and cassettes on topics pertaining to the Integral Way, please write SevenStar Communications, 1314 Second Street, Santa Monica, CA 90401 USA; fax a letter to (310) 917-2267; telephone (310) 576-1901; or mail the enclosed card.

The College of the Integral Way offers teachings on the Integral Way. For a list of Mentors of the Universal Society of the Integral Way in your area or country, or for information about the Integral Way of Life Correspondence Course, please write the College of the Integral Way, 1314 Second Street, Santa Monica, CA 90401 USA; fax to (310) 917-2267; telephone (310) 576-1902; or mail the enclosed card.

Place card in an envelope and mail to:

SEVEN STAR
COMMUNICATIONS
1314 Second Street
Santa Monica, CA 90401 USA

SevenStar Communications Group

Please send me information on the following:

☐ A list of other titles in our series of booklets.

☐ A complete catalog describing books, videos and cassettes on alternative health topics, spiritual realization and movement arts.

☐ A list of Mentors teaching the Integral Way in my area or country.

☐ Information about the Integral Way of Life Correspondence Course.

☐ Chinese regenerative herbal foods for health and longevity.

Name_____

Address_____

City_____ State_____ Zip_____